Reconsidering Abrogation in Islam
Retrieving the Knowledge of Revelation
Leslie Terebessy

Prolegomena 2

Preface 4

Exegesis 5

Fusion of Tradition and Revelation 6

Abrogation 8

    Rationale 9

Reasons for the Application of Abrogation 10

    Atrophy of Reasoning...11

    Tainting of Knowledge... 14

Tawhid.. 15

    Exegesis... 16

Effects of Abrogation... 17

    Penal Law 18

    Prior Revelations.. 19

    Effects in Politics.. 19

Revelation and Abrogation 26

Recommendations 27

Prolegomena

The theory of abrogation is controversial, and with reason. For the application of this theory has enabled tampering with the teaching of revelation.

There is a tendency to assert that the former revelations were corrupted, and that Islam escaped the bane of corruption.

What is missed is that even if the text of revelation remains unchanged, its knowledge may still be corrupted. This is what appears to have transpired, when a few verses of the Quran were pronounced "abrogated."

To declare a verse of revelation to be abrogated is to ask believers to reject a part of revelation, to ask believers to disbelieve in parts of revelation. Is a request of this kind in keeping with the teaching of revelation?

Many jurists rejected abrogation. These encompass Fazlur Rahman, Muhammad Asad, Muhammad 'Abduh, Rashid Rida, and Muhammad Ghazali. Abu Muslim al Isfahani also rejected the theory of abrogation.

The theory of abrogation was adopted to enable an articulation of Islam to justify expeditions to enlarge the "realm of peace" at the expense of the "realm of war," an early variant of the "clash of civilizations" thesis.

The concept of abrogation was adopted to re-interpret Islam in a manner that would justify building an empire.

The teaching of abrogation achieved a political purpose: it facilitated the emergence of "political Islam."

Unfortunately, the application of abrogation tainted the knowledge of revelation. This had adverse effects on the Muslim empire.

That exegetes agreed to the utilization of the theory of abrogation in the first place, to put themselves at the service of a political agenda, is regrettable.

It reveals the plateau which exegesis reached by allowing itself to be used for political ends. It betrays its endorsement of the political authorities of the day.

The theory of abrogation became entrenched after rule of the Mu'tazilites (813 to 849). With the emergence of the prophetic traditions, Islam became "traditional," based on tradition and revelation.

The abrogation of the peace verses by the ayah as-sayf transformed the knowledge of revelation. It transformed the religion of peace into a rationale for empire-building in the "clash" between the "the realm of peace" at the expense of the "realm of war," a process fueled by political aspiration.

The effects of the alteration of the knowledge of revelation are apparent in penal law, where penalties from traditions replaced those prescribed by revelation. The penalties in the traditions flouted the penalties prescribed by revelation. The words of persons "abrogated" the rulings of God.

The application of abrogation by tradition flouted of a fundamental rule of jurisprudence, which is that revelation is the chief authority that may not be abrogated by an alternative authority.

The renewal of Islam requires the rehabilitation of knowledge, in particular, the knowledge of revelation. Hence, what is required is a rehabilitation rather than the Islamization of knowledge. This requires the engagement of reason.

For revelation was "eclipsed" by tradition, facilitated by the teaching of abrogation. Exegesis requires freeing from unwarranted accretions and problematic procedures. The rehabilitation of exegesis, however, requires the utilization and therefore the rehabilitation of reason.

Preface

The renewal of Islamic existence requires the rehabilitation of knowledge. For the Muslim way of life is based on the knowledge of the Muslim way of life. If that knowledge is corrupted, the way of life based on that knowledge will also be tainted. Faced with the necessity to acquire present-day knowledge, Muslims recommend the Islamization of knowledge.

However, what is required is the rehabilitation rather than the Islamization of knowledge. Islam was revealed to be adopted by people. An abstract formula cannot become a Muslim.

Besides, the effort to Islamize knowledge is based upon a faulty presupposition. Revelation does not differentiate between Islamic and unIslamic knowledge. This is a problematic categorization, without foundation in the epistemology of revelation.

A task of greater urgency is the rehabilitation of knowledge. The attainment of knowledge requires the rehabilitation of the method of gaining knowledge. For it was a corruption of the method that explains the corruption of knowledge.

The method of acquiring knowledge of revelation is known as *exegesis* or "explanation." If this method becomes flawed in any way, the results of the procedure will also become flawed.

Recourse to the teaching of abrogation resulted in a corruption of the knowledge of revelation. It facilitated the emergence of an ethos of bellicosity that endorsed expeditions. Eventually, these expeditions ended in a catastrophe.

Exegesis

Exegesis is elucidation. It requires attention. The rules of exegesis are inferred from revelation. All rules require being in accord with revelation. Any assumption that defies revelation is to be examined and, if found wanting, rejected. For results produced by exegesis based on faulty assumption can be expected to be flawed.

That this transpired is reflected in the embedding of the penalties for adultery and apostasy in penal law. For these represent cases where tradition was permitted to "abrogate" revelation thereby tainting penal law. This transpired as the words of persons were allowed to "abrogate" the words of Allah.

Revelation prescribes no punishment for apostasy and a lesser penalty for adultery than tradition. Both penalties depart from revelation. There is no support for these punishments in revelation. Jurists permitted traditions to "abrogate" revelation.

These punishments are taken from tradition on the assumption that tradition may abrogate revelation. This perception is problematic, as it rests on the assumption that persons possess the authority to abrogate the rulings of God.

By enabling rulings from traditions to replace revealed rulings, the practice of abrogation warped the knowledge of revelation. It attributed to it a bellicose character, at variance with its ethos as a teaching of peace. Corruption of knowledge accelerated the waning of Islam.

Renewal accordingly requires a retrieval of the teaching of revelation, unsullied by unwarranted accretions and problematic practices. This requires reconceptualizing exegesis, in particular the problematic foundations on which it rests and the procedures it utilizes.

Fusion of Tradition and Revelation

The acceptance of the theory of abrogation was facilitated by the amalgamation of tradition with revelation. The amalgamation of tradition and revelation took place early in the past. It is being reiterated by neo-traditionalists. These efforts, by their regressive nature, in fact undermine bona fide efforts to renew the Muslim civilization.

These efforts in fact do a disservice to Islam as they peddle what could be termed a version of "textual polytheism," the association if not amalgamation of non-revealed texts with revelation.

The acceptance that reports relayed by persons are "equal" to revelation, the words of Allah "completely conflates the concept of a sahih hadith, sunna, and divine guidance/revelation."[1]

This debacle is a manifestation of the amalgamation of tradition and revelation. Believers are goaded into accepting this notion by being asked to suppress their reason, on the basis of the equally false belief that perceives

---

[1] Adis Duderija, "Bilal Philips as a Proponent of Neo-Traditional Salafism and His Significance for Understanding Salafism in the West," pp. 1 – 22, *Religions*, 2019, 10, 371, doi:10.3390/rel10060371   www.mdpi.com/journal/religions, *Academia*, p. 9, accessed 17 Jan. 2021;

https://www.academia.edu/39398231/Bilal_Philips_as_a_Proponent_of_Neo_Traditional_Salafism_and_His_Significance_for_Understanding_Salafism_in_the_West.

"the use of 'reason-based tafsir' as a form of disbelief (kufr)."[2]

These statements are reiterated by neo-traditionalists in defiance of verses in revelation exhorting believers to "use their reason." It indicates how far they departed from the path they keep exhorting people to follow.

They should begin by first following the advice they proffer to people. These beliefs show how far the knowledge of revelation has been penetrated and corrupted by the misconceptions of tribalism and traditionalism.

Abrogation

The theory of abrogation teaches that a particular text (the abrogator) may, under particular conditions, renders the abrogated text invalid, null and void. These conditions encompass the presence of a disagreement between texts.

The teaching of abrogation is not an article of faith. It was formulated by jurists to resolve what appeared to them as discrepancies in revelation.

---

[2] Adis Duderija, "Bilal Philips as a Proponent of Neo-Traditional Salafism and His Significance for Understanding Salafism in the West," pp. 1 – 22, *Religions*, 2019, 10, 371, doi:10.3390/rel10060371   www.mdpi.com/journal/religions, *Academia*, p. 17, accessed 17 Jan. 2021;

https://www.academia.edu/39398231/Bilal_Philips_as_a_Prop onent_of_Neo_Traditional_Salafism_and_His_Significance_for_ Understanding_Salafism_in_the_West.

Few practices in Islam are as problematic as the theory of abrogation. For it teaches that Allah abrogates His words. It attributes to Allah an aura of uncertainty. It even teaches that persons are able to abrogate the words of God. This perception is beyond audacious. It requires more than just audacity to assert that words of men are able to abrogate the words of God.

Rationale

The theory of abrogation teaches that a verse of revelation may be abrogated by another verse in revelation. This is based on the Quranic verse:

> For whatever sign We change or eliminate or cause to recede into oblivion, We bring forth a better sign, one that is identical. Do you not know that God has power over all things?[3]

As a present-day writer remarked:

> some scholars conclude from the above passage (Q, 2: 106) that certain verses of the Quran have been "abrogated" by God's command before the revelation of the Quran was completed. Apart from the fancifulness of this assertion – which

---

[3] Quran, 2:106, Translated by Muhammad Sarwar, The Quranic Arabic Corpus, accessed on 23 Jun 2020;

http://corpus.quran.com/translation.jsp?chapter=2&verse=106

calls to mind the image of a human author correcting, on second thought, the proofs of his manuscript – deleting one passage and replacing it with another – there does not exist a single reliable Tradition to the effect that the Prophet ever declared a verse of the Quran to have been "abrogated" … In short, the "doctrine of abrogation" has no basis whatever in historical fact, and must be rejected.[4]

In its current form, the theory of abrogation also teaches that a verse of revelation may be abrogated by tradition. This infringes upon the teaching of tawhid, because it suggests that a subordinate authority possesses the ability to abrogate a greater authority.

Reasons for the Application of Abrogation

The acceptance of the theory of abrogation became widespread as a result of the atrophy of reasoning, which reduced ability of exegetes to understand revelation. The deterioration of reasoning resulted from the prohibition of reasoning, inaugurated by the shutting of the gates to

---

[4] Muhammad Asad on the Baseless Concept of 'Abrogation' (Naskh), Uploaded byshees1993
Date uploaded on Aug 01, 2017;
https://www.scribd.com/document/355282325/Muhammad -Asad-on-the-Baseless-Concept-of-Abrogation-Naskh

ijtihad and the following of tradition even against reason, known as taqlid.

Atrophy of Reasoning

After asserting that traditions are needed to "explain" revelation, exegetes asserted that tradition may "abrogate" revelation. Jurists asserted that verses revealed later abrogated verses revealed earlier. The *ayah as-sayf* allegedly abrogated a hundred and twenty peace verses. The allegation that tradition may abrogate revelation amounted to the subordination of revelation to tradition.

The assertion that tradition may abrogate revelation reflects a reversal of the relationship between revelation and tradition. This reversal is also expressed by the sayings that "tradition judges revelation," and that "revelation needs tradition more than tradition needs revelation." The two axioms betray remarkable boldness if not irreverence.

Unfortunately, there are problems with the unitization of tradition to "explain and even "abrogate" revelation. For the assumptions used to justify the engagement of tradition to explain revelation are at variance with the teaching of revelation. The Quran states that it is a "clear" book. Revelation does not say that tradition is revelation.

Revelation rejects abrogation. This is evident in the verses which declare that "there is no changing the words of Allah." The result was that the knowledge of revelation, particularly its teaching of peace, was tainted.

The recourse to abrogation was facilitated by the decline of reasoning. The theory of abrogation was utilized when jurists encountered difficulty in reconciling what appeared to them as inconsistencies in revelation. However, rather than resolving these discrepancies by recourse to reason, they announced that a few verses abrogated related verses. As Muhammad Asad observed:

> At the root of the so-called "doctrine of abrogation" may lie the inability of some of the early commentators to reconcile one Quranic passage with another: a difficulty which was overcome by declaring that one of the verses in question had been "abrogated".[5]

This was an expedient way to resolve the problem, but it produced a bigger problem: that of cancelling entire swathes of revealed verses, thereby distorting the message of revelation and undermining its authority. Hence, the teaching of abrogation has to be discarded.

> This arbitrary procedure explains also why there is no unanimity whatsoever among the upholders of the "doctrine of abrogation" as to which, and how many,

---

[5] Muhammad Asad on the Baseless Concept of 'Abrogation' (Naskh), Uploaded byshees1993 Date uploaded on Aug 01, 2017;

https://www.scribd.com/document/355282325/Muhammad-Asad-on-the-Baseless-Concept-of-Abrogation-Naskh

Quran verses have been affected by it; and, furthermore, as to whether this alleged abrogation implies a total elimination of the verse in question from the context of the Quran, or only a cancellation of the specific ordinance or statement contained in it. In short, the "doctrine of abrogation" has no basis whatever in historical fact and must be rejected.[6]

The difficulty the early jurists had in reconciling various Quranic passages was partly due to the downgrading of reason and the relatively low esteem in which it was held by the partisans of tradition. This was a part of the legacy of the shutting of the doors to ijtihad and the rise of taqlid.

Examination reveals, however, that apparent discrepancies in revelation may be explained, and that there is no necessity to resort to the theory of abrogation. Training in reasoning is required to avoid the necessity to rely upon the theory of abrogation to resolve what appear to be inconsistencies.

---

[6] Muhammad Asad on the Baseless Concept of 'Abrogation' (Naskh), Uploaded byshees1993.

Uploaded on Aug 01, 2017;

https://www.scribd.com/document/355282325/Muhammad-Asad-on-the-Baseless-Concept-of-Abrogation-Naskh

Tainting of Knowledge

The deterioration of reasoning, resulting from the prohibition of juristic ijtihad, made it hard to understand revelation. Jurists began to perceive inconsistencies in revelation and were puzzled about the way to resolve them.

Influenced by anti-rationalism, however, exegetes appealed to tradition rather than reason to "explain" revelation. Yet even tradition has to be understood before it may be used to elucidate revelation. This understanding, as with revelation, is also attained by way of reasoning.

Hence, to think that a person may attain knowledge of either tradition or revelation without the use of reason is less than reasonable. However, even recourse to tradition to explain revelation is problematic, as the prophetic traditions "explain" just a fraction of revelation. The greater part of revelation has no traditions to "explain" it.

When the recourse to tradition to explain revelation did not produce expected results, exegetes resorted to the teaching of abrogation. The engagement of tradition to explain revelation comprised three stages.

First it was announced that revelation has "unclear" passages – a perception that revelation rejects. The second step was to assert that tradition is revelation – a perception also without foundation in revelation.

It appears that exegetes took this step, as verses 5: 44, 45, and 47 prohibit judging by what Allah did not reveal. The third step comprised the assertion that "tradition judges revelation." This perception is also without endorsement in revelation.

The requirement to "judge" revelation by tradition reversed the relationship between tradition and revelation, effectively elevating tradition above revelation.

In this manner, "contradictions" in revelation would be resolved first by recourse tradition and, where tradition unable to reconcile what were perceived as inconsistencies, to the teaching of abrogation.

Tawhid

There are reasons for discarding the theory of abrogation, but none appears as urgent as the requirement to protect tawhid. Whether the theory of abrogation is in accord with tawhid has not received adequate attention.

For tawhid teaches that Allah is without "equals," and that there is "none like unto him."[7] To say that tradition abrogates revelation is to assert that the words of a person are able to abrogate the words of God. This is irreverent.

It presents a challenge to the teaching of tawhid, for to abrogate the words of God would require an authority greater than Allah There is no one greater than God; therefore, there is no authority greater than God. Revelation says:

> God: there is no god but Him, the Ever
> Living, the Ever Watchful. Neither

---

[7] Quran, 112: 4.

slumber nor sleep overtakes Him. All that is in the heavens and in the earth belongs to Him. Who is there that can intercede with Him except by His leave? He knows what is before them and what is behind them, but they do not comprehend any of His knowledge except what He wills. His throne extends over the heavens and the earth; it does not weary Him to preserve them both. He is the Most High, the Tremendous.[8]

It would be presumptuous to think that a person would possess the ability to abrogate the words of God. The problems arising from the theory of abrogation are enough to warrant a fresh enquiry into this problematic theory. Discarding the theory of abrogation would make exegesis manageable.

Exegesis

Tawhid teaches the unity of God. It also teaches that there is nothing like Him. He is Omnipresent, Omniscient, Merciful, Forgiving and All-powerful. Tawhid is the first rule of exegesis.

Yet, when we peruse textbooks on jurisprudence, the term tawhid is distinguished by its absence rather than its

---

[8] Qur'an, 2: 255, p. 29, Translated by M. A. S. Abdel Haleem, Oxford World's Classics, Published in the United States by Oxford University Press Inc., New York, 2005.

presence. We hardly perceive tawhid being referred to, let alone elaborated, and the function it fulfills in jurisprudence.

Every part of jurisprudence requires being in agreement with the teaching of tawhid. To say that a person could abrogate the rulings of God betrays hubris.

It is unthinkable that a person might possesses the power to abrogate the words of His Creator. A person is able to defy the words of Allah but not to abrogate them. The Quran warns against taking people as lords:

> They have taken their rabbis and their priests and the Messiah, son of Mary, for lords besides Allah. And they were not enjoined but that they have none but One Allah to worship. There is no god but He. He is too high in glory, above what they worship besides Him.[9]

In different words, believers are admonished not to take their chiefs as gods.

Effects of Abrogation

Moreover, the teaching of abrogation brought several problems. Firstly, abrogation tainted the knowledge of

---

[9] Quran, 9: 31, trans. by Mohammad Shafi, *Islam Awakened*, accessed 30 Aug. 2020,

https://www.islamawakened.com/quran/9/31/default.htm.

revelation, by abrogating and replacing selected verses with traditions.

Second, as a result of the "abrogation" of the peace verses by the *ayah as-sayf*, abrogation made Islam appear bellicose.

Third, the abrogation of the peace verses endorsed the perspective that fighting has priority in relation to proselytisation.

Fourth, the theory of abrogation warped Islamic legislation by replacing punishments prescribed in revelation by those from traditions.

Abrogation brought a range of adverse effects. These may be perceived in penal law, in foreign relations, in jurisprudence and in politics.

Abrogation altered the teaching of revelation. In Islamic law punishments prescribed by revelation were replaced by punishments from traditions.

Penal Law

An example is the punishment for adultery. Revelation specifies a hundred lashes upon verdict arrived at through the testimony of four reliable witnesses. Tradition calls for stoning to death.

It is hard to see in what way a verse of revelation could be replaced with the words of reporters without injustice to the teaching of tawhid. God's word, it appears, has been abrogated by a person. This appears audacious.

Prior Revelations

Another example is the perception that the Quran abrogated the previous revelations. The Quran states in twenty verses that it *affirms* the previous revelations.[10] How could this perception become entrenched in spite of evidence in revelation to the contrary? It may be that tribal tendencies known as assabiyah played a part on the evolution of "exclusive Islam."

Effects in Politics

Among the political effects of the misunderstanding of revelation were the defeats of Muslims experienced after embarking on foreign expeditions in defiance of revelation according to which "Allah does not love aggressors."

They were encouraged in these expeditions by the politics of exegesis, the misinterpretation of the peace verses to further the political agenda of rulers bent on foreign conquest, encouraged by a political exegesis of revelation, furnished by the application of the teaching of abrogation.

Islamists assert that the peaceful verses in revelation were abrogated by the *ayah as-sayf.* The transformation of the understanding of revelation effected by the alleged abrogation of the peace verses by the *ayah as-sayf* heralded the transformation of the teaching of peace into "political

---

[10] Quran, 2: 41, 87, 89, 91, 97, 101, 3: 3, 50, 81, 4: 47, 5: 48, 6: 92, 10: 37, 12: 111, 35: 31, 37: 37, 41: 43, 46: 9, 12, 30.

Islam." Endorsement for a bellicose articulation of revelation and offensive jihad may be found in:

> *hadith* reports attributed to the Prophet in which he defines the greater jihad (*al-jihad al-akbar*) as a moral and spiritual striving, an internal jihad in which one combats the moral vices and evil tendencies present within one's soul. In contrast other scholars, basing their conclusions on a different set of *hadiths*, proclaim that an offensive jihad (*jihad al-talab*) launched to extend the abode of Islam is valid on religious grounds and, moreover, that it is a collective responsibility (*fard kifayah*) devolving upon all Muslims. If it remains unfulfilled, all of them would be guilty of violating a divine injunction. Undertaking this religious obligation is mandated at least once every year and cannot be neglected, as its importance is equal to observing the obligatory prayers, the Ramadan fast, pilgrimage, and giving

alms. This suggests that it is incumbent upon every adult male. [11]

Islam would be required to engage in campaign to expand the realm of peace at the expense of the realm of war. As a jurist put it:

> the verse (9: 5) does not leave any room in the mind to conjecture about what is called defensive war. This verse asserts that holy war, which is demanded in Islamic law, is not a defensive war because it could legitimately be an offensive war. That is the apex and most honorable of all holy wars. Its goal is the exaltation of the word of God, the construction of Islamic society, and the establishment of God's kingdom on earth regardless of the means. It is legal to carry on an offensive holy war.[12]

---

[11] Hamid Mavani, "Tension between the Quran and the Hadith: The Case of Offensive Jihad," Journal of Shi'a Islamic Studies, Autumn 2011 · Vol. IV · No. 4, p. 398, accessed on 30 May 2018;

<https://serdargunes.files.wordpress.com/2014/09/mavani-tension-between-the-qur_an-and-the-hadith-case-of-offensive-jihad.pdf>

[12] Muhammad Sa'id Ramadan al-Buti, *Jurisprudence in Muhammad's Biography*, Dar al-Fikr, Damascus, 2001, pp. 323 – 4.

It seems that the verse of the sword has been used to promote a militant brand of Islam, hardly consistent with the teaching of revelation. But there is no basis for the abrogation of the peace verses, or any other verses for that matter, in the Quran.

> The term 'sword-verse' is not found in the Quran, or in major Prophetic traditions (hadith). This term represents a later interpretation of the Quran and Islamic law, developed by late eighth/early ninth century religious scholars (ulema), many of whom enjoyed royal patronage. Religious scholars annulled earlier Meccan Quranic verses in favor of the more militant verses revealed in Medina and then rulers employed these verses in Islamic law to legitimate their military jihads of conquest and imperial expansion in the name of defending and spreading Islam.[13]

Hence, the rendition of revelation that sanctions offensive jihad represents a corruption of the knowledge of revelation, resulting from the use of flawed methodology

---

[13] John L. Esposito, "Islam and Political Violence," Religions 2015, 6, 1067–1081; doi: 10.3390/rel6031067, p. 1070; accessed online 30 May 2018;

<www.mdpi.com/2077-1444/6/3/1067/pdf>

and thus requires being treated accordingly. What is required is a rearticulation of tradition. Aa a jurist put it:

> In order to help the Muslim community recover its vision, purposeful-ness, morality, and dynamism, we will need to undertake an earnest, objective, critical reexamination of this community's heritage and history in such a way that we are able to distinguish the good from the bad, the useful from the useless. In so doing, we must not be deterred by cultural taboos, ignorance, clamorous protestations, or material enticements. If we purge our intellectual, educational, and social spheres of weaknesses, prejudices, and distortions, we will be able to nurture an objective, Qur'anically grounded, global perspective...[14]

The acceptance of the theory of abrogation was facilitated by the elevation of tradition to revelation, and its inclusion in the realm of the "sacred." Exegetes attributed sacredness to tradition. This resulted in the veneration of tradition. Unfortunately:

> Muslim intellectuals ... have not been prone to make serious attempts at

---

[14] Abdulhamid A. Abusulayman, *The Qur'anic Worldview: A Springboard for Cultural Reform*, The International Institute of Islamic Thought, 2011, p. 124.

> reforming Muslim thought patterns
> through the critical study and
> examination of their own tradition.[15]

Hence what is required is a critical assessment and a re-evaluation of tradition:

> by means of which one can place Islamic
> tradition under the authority of the
> Qur'an, thereby bringing it into full
> conformity with Qur'anic teachings.[16]

In other words, it is important to ensure that tradition agrees with revelation. Where tradition veers from revelation, tradition becomes unreliable.

Traditional jurists, with the exception of Abu Muslim al-Isfahani and a few others, were reluctant to question abrogation. Present-day jurists, however, appear to have no qualms about it. Muhammad Ghazali, Muhammad Asad, Muhammad 'Abduh, and Rashid Rida, all rejected abrogation. As Muhammad Ghazali states:

---

[15] Abdulhamid A. Abusulayman, *The Qur'anic Worldview: A Springboard for Cultural Reform*, The International Institute of Islamic Thought, 2011, p. 3.

[16] Taha Jabir Alwani, *Apostasy in Islam: A Historical and Scriptural Analysis*, based on the original Arabic translated by Nancy Roberts, The International Institute of Islamic Thought, 2011, p. 6, accessed 28 Dec. 2020;

https://www.academia.edu/43889653/Apostasy_in_Islam_A _Historical_and_Scriptural_Analysis

> The allegation that 120 verses on the invitation to Islam were abrogated by the verse of the sword, is in fact one of crassest stupidity and only serves to show that the great number of Muslims are in a stage of regression of either knowledge or intelligence in our time and have become ignorant of the Qur'an.[17]

As a result of the alleged abrogation of the peaceful verses, Muslim efforts at proselytisation have waned. Indeed, this may be one of the factors for the decline of the Islamic civilization.

> As a result of this ignorance therefore, they have forgotten how to call to the way of God, how to facilitate the call to Islam, and how to be proper examples, and how to present a good perspective. Perhaps this is the reason for the failure in the propagation of Islam, and the prolonged stagnation of the Islamic message being affected – for it has been assumed that the sword is that which fulfills the obligation of delivering the message. Such a concept

---

[17] Muhammad Ghazali, in Khaleel Mohammed, "Muhammad Al-Ghazali's View on Abrogation in the Qur'an," accessed on 11 June, 2020;

http://www.forpeoplewhothink.org/Topics/Abrogation_in_the_Quran.html

is, by the agreement of all those who are rational and discerning, totally absurd. This tale of abrogation then, or the notion of embalming of some verses, in that such verses are present but are inoperative, is a baseless one. There is no verse in the Qur'an which may be said to be out of commission and is therefore now invalid; this is nonsense...There is no contradiction in the Qur'an whatsoever, for every verse has a context within which it functions.[18]

Nevertheless, to this day we encounter arguments who assert that the teaching of abrogation is an essential part of the faith, and even that those who do not believe in it abandoned their faith. This takes a measure of audacity.

Revelation and Abrogation

Revelation does not support the theory of abrogation. It says that "there is no changing the words of Allah."

They shall have good news in this world's life and in the hereafter; there is no

---

[18] Muhammad Ghazali, in Khaleel Mohammed, "Muhammad Al-Ghazali's View on Abrogation in the Qur'an," accessed on 11 June, 2020;

http://www.forpeoplewhothink.org/Topics/Abrogation_in_t he_Quran.html

changing the words of Allah; that is the mighty achievement.[19]

And the word of your Lord has been accomplished truly and justly; there is none who can change His words, and He is the Hearing, the Knowing.[20]

And recite what has been revealed to you of the Book of your Lord, there is none who can alter His words; and you shall not find any refuge besides Him.[21]

These verses constitute evidence that the theory of abrogation has no basis in revelation and therefore that it rests on a weak foundation.

Recommendations

It is evident that the teaching of abrogation is problematic and represents an aberration in exegesis and jurisprudence. The theory generates misunderstanding and enables unscrupulous persons to warp the teaching of revelation,

---

[19] Quran, 10: 64, *Islam Awakened*, translated by Muhammad Habib Shakir, accessed online on 5 July 2020, https://www.islamawakened.com/quran/10/64/default.htm.

[20] Quran, 6:115, *Islam Awakened*, translated by Muhammad Habib Shakir, accessed online on 5 July 2020, https://www.islamawakened.com/quran/6/115/default.htm.

[21] Quran, 18:27, *Islam Awakened*, translated by Muhammad Habib Shakir, accessed online on 5 July 2020, https://www.islamawakened.com/quran/18/27/default.htm.

by imparting to it a bellicose tenor, supportive of the agenda of expansion.

For this reason, it is necessary to revisit the teaching of abrogation to determine whether it is in agreement with revelation. The renewal of the Islamic civilization requires rehabilitation of the knowledge of revelation, which was tainted by problematic practices as the teaching of abrogation. This requires the rehabilitation of exegesis which was responsible for the alteration of the knowledge of revelation by its utilization of the theory of abrogation.

Printed in Great Britain
by Amazon

28579280R00018